Yao Ming

Yao Ming

Michael Bradley

BENCHMARK BOOKS

MARSHALL CAVENDISH
NEW YORK

Benchmark Books
Marshall Cavendish
99 White Plains Road
Tarrytown, NY 10591-9001
www.marshallcavendish.com

Library of Congress Cataloging-in-Publication Data

Bradley, Michael, 1962–
Yao Ming / by Michael Bradley.
p. cm.—(Benchmark all-stars)
Summary: Discusses the personal life and basketball career of the Houston Rockets
center. Includes bibliographical references and index.
ISBN 0-7614-1758-3
1. Yao, Ming 1980—Juvenile literature. 2. Basketball players—China—Biography—
Juvenile literature. [1. Yao, Ming 1980– 2. Basketball players.] I. Title II. Series: Bradley,
Michael, 1962– . Benchmark all-stars.

GV884.Y66B73 2003
796.323'092—dc22

2003022948

Photo Research by Regina Flanagan

Cover: AP/Wide World Photos

Robert Seale/TSN/Icon Sports Media: 2–3; Richard Carson/Reuters: 6, 8, 10, 31;
AFP/Corbis: 9, 14, 23, 29, 35; AP/Wide World Photos: 12, 24, 28, 30, 32, 36, 37, 38,
40, 43, 44; Kevin R. Morris/Bohemian Nomad Picturemakers/Corbis: 16; Corbis: 17;
Macduff Everton/Corbis: 18; Sergio Perez/Reuters: 20; Al Tielemans/Sports Illustrated:
22; Sue Ogrocki/Reuters: 26; Reuters: 41; Tim Shaffer/Reuters: 42.

Series design by Becky Terhune

Printed in Italy

1 3 5 6 4 2

Contents

Yao Ming and Shaquille O'Neal smile and shake hands before their first match.

CHAPTER ONE

The Big Showdown

He had mocked him. Just six months before, Shaquille O'Neal, the NBA's biggest big man, had taken some shots. He questioned whether Yao Ming would be successful. He even made fun of the 7'5" Chinese center's native language

"Tell Yao Ming, 'Ching, chong yang wah ah so.'"

Even though the mighty Shaq had apologized in Yao's Mandarin dialect—"dui bu qi" (meaning, "I'm sorry")—the message had been clear. Shaq didn't respect Yao. He didn't think he belonged in the National Basketball Association (NBA). He certainly wasn't too happy with all the attention Yao received after the Houston Rockets made him the first overall pick in the 2002 draft, the first foreign player ever to be so honored. When the two finally met on the basketball court on January 17, 2003, the basketball world was in full frenzy.

Houston's first game against Shaq's Los Angeles Lakers lacked similar drama. That's because the 7'1" O'Neal had been out of the lineup with an injured toe. Yao took full advantage of O'Neal's absence by making all nine of his shots and scoring 20 points. That was impressive. If Yao were to do it against Shaq, it would be amazing.

Even though Shaq was all business before the game, he did make a gesture of peace to Yao before the opening tip-off, telling him, "I love you. We are brothers." Yao then proceeded to act like a bullying older sibling by swatting away three of Shaq's shots in the game's first five minutes. It was a forceful statement by a man not known for drawing attention to himself. Yao could hang with the big boys. And though he scored 10 points to Shaq's 31 and had just ten *rebounds* to his rival's thirteen, Yao had proven he belonged. Of his six blocked shots, five came at the expense of Shaq. After the game—which Houston won, 108-104, in overtime—Yao was quite respectful of Shaq, despite the previous trouble. "We're all basketball players," he said. "We all live together on this earth."

Yao's words of peace stood in stark contrast to the wild swirl of attention that surrounded his first year in the NBA. He had bridged the deep *cultural* gap between America and China in spectacular fashion. Few, if any, other players have made such a dramatic entrance into the league. Not even Michael Jordan arrived with such fanfare. From the moment Yao staged his first official workout for NBA scouts, coaches,

Houston Rockets center Yao Ming blocks Shaquille O'Neal's opening shot in their first game, sending the Lakers' top man to the floor.

and general managers, he was a full-fledged phenomenon. And once he started to prove that he was more than just a tall curiosity from a strange land, Yao received even more attention. The Rockets didn't make the playoffs, but Yao's final statistical averages (13.5 points per game, 8.2 rebounds per game, 1.8 blocks per game) demonstrated his talent and the potential for greater future success.

Even the NBA fraternity, which regards newcomers with suspicion, embraced him. Yao's Houston teammates warmed to him quickly. "It's hard to describe what Yao has meant," Rockets guard Cuttino Mobley said. "But it's been great—I mean great—having him around." And after Shaq's first silly remarks, the other league stars stepped up to welcome the new guy. "He's special," Philadelphia 76ers guard Allen Iverson said. "He's a gift from God."

Houston's Chinese community was thrilled to have him land in their town.

Houston Rockets' Yao Ming dunks against the Lakers.

Los Angeles Lakers center Shaquille O'Neal elbows Yao Ming in the nose during overtime of their first game. The Houston Rockets won, 108-104.

Every Rockets game featured large groups of Chinese fans. Concession stands at the Compaq Center offered Asian food. There were half-time performances featuring Chinese athletes and entertainers. The impact was similar around the league. Everywhere Yao went, Asian fans came out to show their support. This was not just a new basketball phenomenon. For many Americans, it was an entirely new face on Chinese culture.

"Yao has given a new Chinese image," China *Sports Weekly* reporter Xi Kiaohe told *Sports Illustrated*. "People thought of Chinese people as short and skinny, not fierce, unable to play competitive sports. Yao has shown that is wrong. But he [has] also stayed kind and friendly and warm. I think a lot of people know that about him now."

Yao met every interview request and press conference with the same grace and straightforward approach. He even mixed some humor into his answers. After telling reporters before the Lakers game that he had invited Shaq to his house for dinner, he added that he was afraid his refrigerator wasn't large enough to handle the Big Fella's appetite. Everywhere Yao went, he patiently answered questions. The same questions. But he didn't snap at reporters or act aloof. And when he did have free time, he indulged his love of pizza, ribs, and chicken wings—in addition to his beloved spicy Szechuan fare (when he could find it). He slept. A lot. And he became one of the largest collectors of action video games and DVDs. With each day, Yao was becoming more and more comfortable in America.

"He's just like me, only 7'5" and Chinese," Rockets guard Steve Francis said.

And an international sensation.

Yao's incredible height marked him as a likely basketball player from youth. So did the height and talent of his parents, who also played basketball. Here, he towers over a coach.

CHAPTER TWO

First Steps

Knuckles. It all started with Yao's knuckles. It was 1993. Yao was thirteen years old and had already soared to more than 6' tall. When Yao's knuckles were measured—a common practice in China—the conclusion was dramatic. He would be a giant at twenty.

In America that might have led to heightened interest from local high school coaches or summer-league teams. In China, it was different. Yao's height—and that of his parents—attracted the attention of the national governing body of athletics, which was responsible for making sure all Chinese teams that competed against other squads from other countries were strong. Unlike the United States, where each different sport is run by a separate organization, all Chinese athletics come under the rule of the country's one national governing group. So, here was a tall boy with tall parents. That could add up to big things for China.

China is quite unlike America—in many ways. One of the largest differences is in our forms of government. While the United States is a democracy, in which the people vote for their leaders, China is a communist state. That means rulers rise to power, and the country's 1.2 billion people have little say in the matter. Most leaders are appointed by Communist Party officials, who have moved into positions of higher authority through loyalty to the party. Many remain in their positions for decades. The Chinese people must do as their leaders say or risk some hard consequences, such as going to jail or being sent to live

The fame of U.S. superstar Michael Jordan helped make basketball the fastest growing sport in many Asian countries, including China, where Yao grew up.

away from their families in other parts of the country. So, when a teenager sprouts to 6'2" or 6'3", the Chinese sports authorities become interested. He could be a valuable asset in the country's constant push to promote its way of life and communist form of government. Through the success of its people, Chinese leaders hope that other countries will become communist themselves. They believe that if Chinese sports teams are successful, the world will see that the country's system of government is successful.

It was predicted that Yao would soar to 7'4"—or taller. So much for leading a regular life. Yao was assigned to a special academy designed to cultivate athletes. Though he was still in his hometown of Shanghai, where he was born in 1980, Yao was on a special path. "It felt like I was starting out on my own for the first time," Yao said.

A Brief History of China

The long history of China dates back more than 7,000 years and is generally considered to have begun officially in the twenty-first century B.C.E. with the Xia Dynasty. The Chinese were pioneers in many different skills, from language development to animal husbandry to warfare and commerce.

Chinese influence and land grew throughout the dynasties of the first millennium, and peaked as the Mongols, warrior tribes from the interior of China, began to conquer societies across Asia and into Europe. At one point, the Mongols controlled nearly all of what is now considered Russia, in addition to most of the Asian lands.

By the late fourteenth century, the Ming Dynasty dawned. It may have been China's most recognized period. Beijing became the country's capital, and the Mongols' power and influence lessened greatly. The Qing Dynasty followed, beginning in 1644, when the Manchus to the north took power. This was China's last imperial dynasty.

In 1911, China became a republic under the rule of Sun Yat-sen. And though China had considerable land and a large population, it struggled with the Japanese, who had for centuries sought to exercise influence over their neighbors. Sun Yat-sen died in the 1920s and was replaced by Chiang Kai-shek, who ruled until China became a communist state in 1949.

Mao Zedong led the revolution that brought communism to China. Mao held supreme power in the communist state, which was built on the idea that all people were equal, and that no one should have more wealth or influence than anyone else. That sounded great, but it was hard to put into practice, especially in a country as big as China. The vast majority of the people were poor, while a select group became rich and comfortable. Anyone who dared to criticize Mao or the state was put in prison or killed. The state controlled all of the newspapers and even had final approval on works of art or literature.

Chiang, meanwhile, fled to the nearby island of Taiwan, where he continued to rule the republic. Mao governed the People's Republic of China on mainland China until his death in 1976. Since that time, a succession of rulers has led the country, beginning with Deng Xiaoping, after Mao. Today, China's president is Hu Jintao, who has instituted many economic reforms but remains true to Mao's communist vision. While the people have more freedom to make better lives for themselves, they still have limited rights and still cannot criticize the government or leave the country freely.

A group of Chinese students play basketball at West China University.

It made sense that he played basketball. His father, Yao Zhiyuan, is 6'7" and was a member of the Chinese national men's basketball team. His mother, Fang Fengdi, who is 6'3", played on the women's team. In addition to playing ball, each had good jobs when Yao was growing up. His father was an engineer with the Shanghai harbor administration, which makes sure the ships that sail to and from the city do so in an orderly fashion and without breaking any laws. His mother was a high-ranking official in the Chinese sports-research institute. They exposed Yao to basketball at an early age. "When I first started playing basketball, everybody was bigger than me," Yao said. That didn't last too long.

Basketball has only recently enjoyed considerable popularity in China. Table tennis, or Ping-pong, is China's national pastime, the equivalent of baseball in the United States. Soccer is the next most preferred sport. And basketball ranks third. Of course, thanks to Yao's success during the 2002–2003 NBA season, more and more people are playing and watching the sport.

Shanghai, the
city where Yao
grew up.

But it is not as if basketball is a new pursuit for China. The country first started bouncing the orange ball in 1908, through the Shanghai YMCA. Fifteen years later, a college student named Dong Shou Yi studied the game in Massachusetts with its inventor, Dr. James Naismith. Though the Chinese had national teams through the 1940s and 1950s, those outfits did not have very talented players and competed—with marginal success—only against other communist countries. In the 1990s, however, the NBA began to promote its game in China, looking to attract the attention of the world's most heavily populated country. In 1995, the Chinese Basketball Association was formed, and interest in basketball grew.

"When I first started playing basketball, everybody was bigger than me."
—Yao Ming

17

A poster at a bus stop in Hong Kong features the U.S.A. basketball "Dream Team" that Yao Ming played against in 2000. He was overwhelmed by the talent of the U.S. players, but that strengthened his determination to excel.

A Chinese Basketball Association (CBA) team—the Shanghai Sharks—signed Yao to his first professional contract, at age fifteen. Unlike the NBA, which *mandates* that players must have graduated high school and be at least eighteen years of age to play in the league, the CBA often drafts younger teenagers. Those players then work and practice with the team and are cultivated for full-time play as they get older. That's what happened with Yao.

As he grew, so did the CBA. Shanghai, a team co-owned by the government and some local business owners, became a powerhouse. And Yao was growing taller and more capable as a player. The Chinese basketball world was learning about him and what he would be able to accomplish some day. It was time for the rest of the planet to become exposed to Yao. In the coming years, he would make a huge impression on hoops experts and spark debate about whether he had the talent to play in the NBA—and whether the Chinese government would ever let him.

Yao had taken his first steps. It was time to start running.

Vince Carter of the United States dunks off an ally oop pass over China's Yao Ming during the 2000 Olympic Games in Australia.

CHAPTER THREE
Making an Impression

This was his chance. His chance to shine. The Chinese government had decided that Yao would not be allowed to play in the 2000 Hoops Summit, the annual game that pits the best U.S. high school seniors against the best eighteen-and-under players from around the world. That was a setback. But here Yao was on an even bigger stage—the 2000 Summer Olympics, in Sydney, Australia.

It was his opportunity to show the world what he could do. His chance to help China's basketball program become important on the world stage. Here he was, all of twenty years old, and the international hoops community was eager to see how he would do against the best there was: the *U.S. Dream Team*. Though China's "Walking Great Wall" also included 7' tall forwards Wang Zhizhi and Menk Bateer, Yao was clearly the center of attention. Everybody wanted to see what this 7'5" giant could do. Was he as skilled as everybody said? Could he dribble and pass like a man more than a foot smaller? How would he do against the likes of NBA *frontcourt* stars Kevin Garnett, Alonzo Mourning, and Antonio McDyess?

Yao couldn't wait. "I've been looking forward to this match for a long time," he said. Ever since the move to keep him out of the Hoops Summit—a decision that upset him— Yao had been eager to play against American competition. Tearing up the CBA was one

Chinese Basketball Association's Yao Ming plays defense!

thing. Doing it against the best in the world was quite another. The decision to keep Yao out of the Hoops Summit had been a typical Chinese standoff. Yao wanted to play, but his country's government was concerned that giving him a taste of Western culture might lead him to seek an opportunity to play for the NBA. So, Chinese national team coach Jiang Xingquan moved up the country's Olympic training schedule by a week, closing the gap between the end of Yao's CBA campaign and the workouts. When Yao complained—politely—that he should be allowed to play in the Hoops Summit, he was told that he needed rest following the CBA season. "I'm not that tired," he said later to reporters.

There was nothing to keep him from the Olympics. China wanted to be there, to show that its basketball program had made great strides since 1996, when the United States walloped China, 133-71, at the Olympics in Atlanta. But that was without Yao. Things would be different in 2000.

Or would they?

It was clear to anybody who saw Yao play that he wasn't just a giant. He was a giant basketball player. "He's very good, very skilled," said Garnett, a smooth 7'-tall power forward. But Yao struggled against the faster, stronger Americans. He finished with 5 points and 3 rebounds in the 119-72 blowout loss. He struggled with *foul* trouble and discovered that he was not yet ready to think about playing—and succeeding—in the NBA. Perhaps the Chinese basketball bosses were right to keep him within the country's borders. Yao wasn't ready for the big time yet. "We learned a lot from this game," Yao said afterward. "The United States team is very experienced," he noted.

New Zealand's Sean Marks blocks an attempt at a shot by China's Yao Ming during the Olympics.

That is not to say Yao was not making progress. He first came over to the United States in 1998, to a training camp in Oregon sponsored by Nike, the shoe manufacturer. Yao attracted attention because of his size, but it was clear he had some work to do. By 2000, he had made noticeable improvement.

"The biggest one, that 7'5" guy, I met him a while back, and he was really weak then, not aggressive enough," said Dream Team guard Tim Hardaway, who first encountered Yao in 1995 at an international youth camp in Paris. "But he's developed a lot since then. He can play."

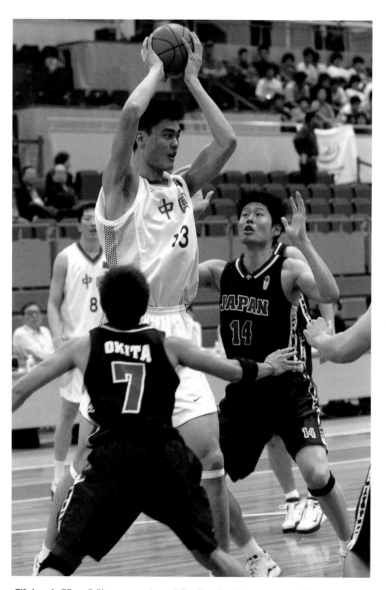

China's Yao Ming soars with the ball over two Japanese players during the men's semifinal match at the Third East Asian Games in Osaka, Japan, in May 2001.

Yao was better, but he was not coming to the NBA any time soon. That was not just because he wasn't ready. China was trying to keep its best players at home, for fear that letting them visit the United States would lead the stars to stay away. They wouldn't come back to train with the national team. Worse, they would fall in love with the West and want to stay. That was not the best advertisement for the Chinese system. Wang Zhizhi was trying to get his *clearance*, but the government was not willing to give it. If he couldn't go, there was no way Yao, who was only twenty, would get permission. So, he stayed in Shanghai, playing for the Sharks. He earned only $20,000 a year. He had to wash his own uniform and put up with life in a cramped dormitory. Though Nike had signed him to an endorsement contract worth $200,000 over four years, Yao was clearly worth more. Even if he earned one of the top salaries in the Chinese Basketball Association, it would not come close to a top NBA payday.

When his salary jumped to $70,000 a year in 2001, it was still well below the millions

The NBA Draft

The NBA draft is nearly as old as the league itself, but it has undergone significant changes since it began, just before the 1947–1948 season, in the NBA's second year.

The original purpose of the draft, the one that still holds today, was to provide the league's less-successful teams with a way to improve. The team that finished with the worst record in a certain season received the first selection among college players who had spent four years on campus. The second-worst team chose next. And so on.

That practice continued for nearly forty years, with few variations. For a period, teams were allowed to make territorial picks, which let them secure the services of a player who spent his college days at a school near the team. In 1962, for instance, the Detroit Pistons chose Dave DeBusschere, a forward from the University of Detroit.

The 1970s brought changes. In 1976, the NBA allowed players who had not completed four years of college to make themselves eligible for the draft. In 1985, the league became concerned that teams were losing on purpose to secure better draft picks, so it instituted the lottery system, which continues today. The names of each team that did not make the playoffs were put into a container, and a league representative chose which team would select first and so on. The lottery was adjusted almost annually from that point on, with the worst teams getting a better chance at the top pick, but with no guarantees that finishing at the bottom would yield the top choice.

that awaited him in the NBA. And Yao wanted to make the move. Earlier in 2001, China had allowed Wang to move to America to play for the Dallas Mavericks, which had drafted him in 1999 and had gone through long negotiations to convince the Chinese to allow Wang to play in the NBA. Now it was Yao's turn. Most agreed he would be the first overall pick in the draft. His 7'5" frame had filled out naturally, distributing nearly 300 pounds evenly. He could shoot the *three-pointer* and dribble and pass like some guards. He was ready. But China wasn't. A few days after Wang headed to Dallas, CBA director Xin Lancheng declared, "Yao will not be going this year." The dream was put on hold.

Yao Ming was the first foreign player who had not played at a U.S. university ever to be selected number one in the NBA draft.

CHAPTER FOUR

Coming to America

It was a simple declaration, not made in the best English but certainly understandable to all who heard it.

"Hi Houston and everybody. I come."

After nearly two years of deal making, near misses and false starts, Yao had made it to the NBA. On Draft Day, 2002, the Houston Rockets used the first overall pick to take the Chinese center. Yao had become the first-ever international player to be the top choice. "This is now a new start in my basketball life," Yao said. "This is a new league in front of me to play in, so it will be a challenge to me."

After what it took to get Yao to the NBA, some might have wondered whether there was anything more challenging. Though the real on-court work lay ahead, the process by which Yao was released from his Shanghai Sharks was certainly not easy. The NBA had not reached a formal agreement with the Chinese Basketball Association until 11 P.M. the day before the draft. Only, there was a problem: The agreement was written in Chinese. Two hours later, an English copy was faxed to the Rockets, who were then clear to draft Yao. The *franchise* was thrilled, and not just because Yao represented a chance to win games. This was an historic event, linking together two countries that hadn't always been the best of friends.

"We think this guy can bring us championships, along with the other players we have," Rockets owner Les Alexander said. "But this is more than just a sports story."

The NBA-China Deal for Yao

The first call came a few days after the Houston Rockets were awarded the first pick in the 2002 NBA Draft. Team officials contacted Chinese representatives to see if Yao would be allowed to play in the NBA.

The negotiations were delicate. China viewed Yao as its property, a person whose talents would help spread the communist message across the world. If China were to become a basketball power, thanks to Yao, people would see how successful communism was. So, when negotiations began, the Chinese were going to demand a lot.

The final deal was one both sides could live with. Houston paid China a $350,000 fee for Yao's rights. That is the highest amount allowed by the NBA. It is usually paid to a foreign player's team, but in this case it went to the Chinese government. It was determined that at least 50 percent of Yao's contract earnings would go to China. If Yao becomes a star, that could ultimately be $5 million to $8 million a year.

China also demanded that Yao continue to fulfill most of his national team obligations. If that meant he would be practicing and playing in tournaments right up to the start of the regular season, so be it. In 2003, Yao missed the first two weeks of training camp to play with the Chinese national team. It was a hard bargain, but in the end, the NBA and Yao were big winners.

Yao Ming—chosen for the NBA but still playing in China—cheers his teammates.

Several factors delayed the agreement's completion. One was the question of when Yao would be available for service to Houston. Because the Asian games were scheduled to be held in October, China did not want its star center to participate in a training camp at the time. It wanted Yao to play for his homeland. So, Houston permitted Yao to miss all of camp and some of the preseason. The same would go for future international competitions. If China called, Yao would have to answer, even if it meant he might miss some *crucial* development with his team and the chance to become better prepared for the NBA game. It didn't matter. Houston felt Yao was worth it.

"We have a very athletic player who can do a lot of things," said then-Houston coach Rudy Tomjanovich, who coached the 2000 American Olympic team that whipped Yao and his Chinese team. "He runs well, passes well, shoots well. What I really like about him, besides all those things, is his philosophy. His head is on straight. His No. 1 priority is the team."

Yao says goodbye to his father and mother as he heads back to national team training camp.

Houston Rockets assistant coach Mike Wells goes over a play with Yao Ming during a presentation game against the Philadelphia 76ers.

The final deal that brought Yao to the NBA was not an easy one to negotiate. It seemed that Yao and a sports agent named Michael Coyne had an agreement. In 1999, Yao negotiated a contract with Coyne that would have transferred nearly 33 percent of Yao's NBA salary to various government and basketball concerns in China. That may sound like Yao gave back a lot, but it was better than what Yao eventually agreed to in 2002, in which 50 percent of his money went back home.

But the Rockets didn't care about what money was going where. They wanted Yao the player—the man they saw average 38.8 points and 20.2 rebounds per game in the 2002 CBA playoffs. The man they saw improve his free throw shooting percentage from 48.5 percent his first year with Shanghai to 74.9 percent in 2001–2002. The man they saw demonstrate considerable skills during a pre-draft workout at Chicago's Loyola College, which was attended by one hundred fifty media members and seventy NBA representatives. During that showcase, Yao showed he could nail three-pointers with ease, had smooth *low-post* moves, and could *execute* the kind of two- and three-step drills that sometimes trip up giant players. It was the first time most people had seen Yao, and while he was largely successful, the reviews were still mixed.

"He runs well, passes well, shoots well. What I really like about him, besides all those things, is his philosophy. His head is on straight. His No. 1 priority is the team."
—Rudy Tomjanovic

Houston Rockets fans spell out Y-A-O!

Los Angeles Clippers guard Quentin Richardson liked what he saw of Yao but was careful to add that the workout did not take place with NBA players. Yao worked with a couple of college players and some NBA assistant coaches. "He impressed everyone," Richardson said. "But I think if you switched all these faces, and these were guys in the [NBA] sitting here, actual NBA players, they would not be as impressed." Richardson's message was clear: shooting and running and jumping did not make a real NBA player. You need more. The drills were run by P. J. Carlesimo, a former NBA coach and current assistant with San Antonio. He echoed Richardson's sentiments. "The one thing about the NBA I don't think anyone understands is the athletic ability, the size, the strength and quickness of the players," Carlesimo said. "It's at another level."

Yao did have his supporters. Golden State Warriors general manager Garry St. Jean liked what he saw. "He has a feel for the game, particularly in passing and shooting. You can see it's come along very nicely."

On Draft Day, Houston wasn't worried about Yao's strength. The Rockets didn't care that he might miss some training camp or that he had a huge cultural gap to bridge. The team was thrilled to have Yao, just as Yao was thrilled to be an NBA player.

"The whole franchise wanted this so badly," Houston general manager Carroll Dawson said.

Yao had made it to America. It was time to play ball. Finally.

Yao Ming dunks a ball to score against the Phoenix Suns.

CHAPTER FIVE

Early Reviews

It was not the most impressive debut. Even though the basketball world had been anxious to see Yao finally play in the NBA, his early performances didn't exactly inspire confidence in his supporters.

Part of the problem was his arrival time. Instead of taking part in a full training camp, during which he could learn Houston's system, develop bonds with his teammates, and discover how physical and athletic NBA players were, Yao came to the United States nine days before the 2002–2003 season began. And even if he had been able to step right in and handle his basketball career, he still faced the huge tasks of getting used to a new culture, a new country, and a new language. Yao was way behind, and on opening night against Indiana, it showed.

With six million Chinese watching a satellite broadcast of the game, Yao didn't score a point in eleven minutes of action. He had more fouls (three) than rebounds (two). Houston fell, 91-82, to the Pacers, and the big newcomer appeared *tentative* and overmatched. "I still have a lot to learn," Yao said. "It's a very long road, and it's difficult." Although the Rockets' officials jumped to Yao's defense—"The guy's been here ten days," then-coach Rudy Tomjanovich said—it appeared as if the rookie was in for quite a shock.

There had been tremendous anticipation about his arrival. Everybody had been impressed with Yao during his workout back in late April, but running through drills was one thing. Playing against the world's best was another. Yao seemed to handle his first week in America well. He impressed Tomjanovich with his commitment to the team. "One thing I like about him is that he's humble, and he's uncomfortable with all of this attention," Tomjanovich said. "He wants to be treated like any other Rocket." Yao's teammates appreciated that and also were happy to see that the big newcomer was a quick learner. Whenever something new was presented to him, Yao picked it up quickly. By January, he was even teaching his teammates. During one timeout in a game against Phoenix, Yao took the clipboard from a coach and diagrammed the proper footwork for a particular defensive assignment.

He was making progress, but it was hard to measure. Things didn't improve quickly after the shaky opener. Yao averaged less than 4 points a game in his first six contests. He was often out of position on defense and had trouble getting his shot off at the other end. In a game against the Phoenix Suns, guard Stephon Marbury worked a *crossover move* that confused Yao so much that he fell to the floor after tripping over his own tangled feet. Making matters worse was the media attention that accompanied his every move. Yao had to endure pre-game press conferences, post-game briefings, and off-day sessions. Whenever the Rockets traveled to a new city, there was a flood of attention. Meanwhile, some fans kept a close eye on him, and some even waited for failure. "I thought there would be a lot of media, but I never thought there would be this many," he said. "I wouldn't say I'm sick of the media, but it does annoy me."

It was a tough start to a dream. Then, as if by magic, the skies brightened. In November, he exploded against Dallas, which had its own giant center, 7'6" Shawn Bradley. Yao finished with 30 points and 16 rebounds. Some were impressed, but the Mavericks weren't exactly known for their defense, and Bradley isn't exactly an All-Star. So, Yao did more.

International Players in the NBA

Yao Ming's status as the first foreign-born player with no U.S. ties ever to be the top pick in the NBA draft was a milestone, but it was just the latest step in the growing international presence in the league. For most of the first thirty-five years of the NBA's history, American players dominated rosters. But as the 1970s turned into the 1980s, players from other countries also began to find their way to the top.

One of the earliest international stars was Hakeem Olajuwon, a Nigerian who played at the University of Houston and was drafted by the Houston Rockets first overall in 1984. Other 1980s foreign players included German Detlef Schrempf, 7'7" Sudanese center Manute Bol, and Lithuanian guard Sarunas Marciulionis.

The world came to the NBA in even greater numbers in the 1990s, and by the end of the decade, scouts and personnel executives were flocking to Europe in search of new talent. Today, there are players from many different countries (Yugoslavia, Russia, Lithuania, Germany, Argentina, Brazil, France, Croatia, Mexico, Canada, and even England among them) in the league, and each year brings more and more talent from abroad—like Yao Ming.

Each player who becomes part of an NBA team retains his citizenship. Yao is still a Chinese citizen, even though he is part of the Houston Rockets. If he wanted to become an American, he would have to go through the same process as any other person who left his country to become a United States citizen. Were Yao to defect and ask to become an American, his family and friends in China would face punishment from the government, which does not allow its people to leave the country freely.

Yao Ming slam dunks two of his first twenty-one first-half points against the Dallas Mavericks.

Almost all of the international players who join the NBA keep their salaries and any money they make from endorsements. Yao is different. He must give a large portion (more than 50 percent) of his salary to the Chinese government. He may buy whatever he wants with whatever is left over, although China does not have as many stores and products available as does the United States. When he is in America, though, Yao spends his money on the items he enjoys.

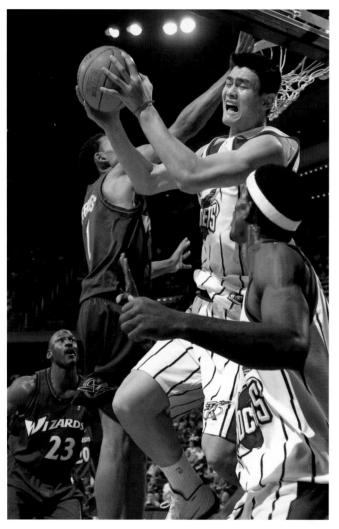

Yao Ming grabs a rebound from Washington Wizards' Jared Jeffries.

Against 7'-tall Tim Duncan of San Antonio, a perennial All-Star who was to be the 2002–2003 NBA Most Valuable Player, Yao scored 27 points and hauled down 18 rebounds. He was beginning to get it.

And he was attracting new admirers with almost every game. Playing Orlando in early January, Yao found himself in the corner with the ball, and the *shot clock* running down. Magic center Pat Burke was crowding him, trying to force a *turnover* or bad pass. So, Yao leaned against Burke, spun quickly, and scored on a soft *finger roll*. It was a tremendous example of Yao's game. He didn't panic. Instead, he used his skill and size to turn a potential problem into two points. "Two steps, and he is at the basket," Burke said afterward, still amazed. "I tell you what, I won't trap him in the corner again. I did not think he could put it on the floor like that. I guess he proved me wrong."

Yao was even becoming more comfortable

with the aggressive side of the NBA game. When Houston general manager Carroll Dawson met with Yao after the Rockets drafted him, he explained that Yao had to become

"I did not think he could put it on the floor like that. I guess he proved me wrong."
—Orlando Magic center Pat Burke

more willing to dunk the ball. That's considered bad sportsmanship in China, but in the NBA, it has to be done. Players who don't go to the basket strongly will have their shots blocked by smaller defenders. So, Yao started dunking. Against Atlanta in December, he even received a technical foul for screaming at Hawks center Theo Ratliff after dunking on him. It may not have been the most gentlemanly play, but it signaled that Yao was becoming more and more comfortable with the NBA game.

And things were going to get even better.

Yao Ming shoots the ball past Milwaukee Bucks' Ervin Johnson.

Orlando Magic's Tracy McGrady drives on Ming under the basket during the 2003 NBA All-Star game on February 9, 2003.

CHAPTER SIX

Yao-Mania

By January 2003, Yao had it all going in the right direction. He had become completely comfortable with life in the NBA, although the *avalanche* of media attention hadn't slowed one bit. And the league's fans were responding to his excellent play. Not only were they turning out for his games—home and away—they were also giving him considerable status.

When all the fans' votes were counted for the Western Conference starters in the 2003 All-Star game in Atlanta, Yao had been elected the first-team center, over Shaquille O'Neal, the usual choice. It was big news. Here was Yao, a rookie from a far-off land, grabbing a spot on the West's first five from Shaq, one of the NBA's biggest stars, in what was essentially a popularity contest. In Yao's typical humble fashion, he said he didn't deserve to be elected. "But I would like to thank the fans for voting for me," he said.

Yao may not have been as happy with the fans' support two days before the game, when he marched into the Centennial Ballroom at the Hyatt Regency Hotel in Atlanta for the annual All-Star press conference. Each player was given a specific table at which he would sit and answer questions. When Yao arrived, he was stunned to see that more reporters and camera operators had gathered around him than any other player. Here was the cream of the NBA, and Houston rookie center Yao Ming of China was the biggest draw. "I would like to leave this place as soon as possible," he said early on in the interview. No such luck.

For nearly an hour, he answered all the questions, most of which had been posed to him dozens of times before. His favorite off-court pursuit? Sleep. His biggest influence as a young player? Houston center Hakeem Olajuwon. The toughest thing about the NBA? "The biggest adaptation to the NBA is to play games consecutively, back-to-back," he said. "But I don't think it is a problem only for the international players."

Yao had indeed hit something of the "rookie wall," that imaginary barrier that gets in the way of first-year players who aren't used to the pace of play, the travel, or the amount of games. But he was still going strong. In February, he was named the Western Conference's Rookie of the Month, thanks to his averages of 16.5 points and 8.8 rebounds per game. Yao was a big part of Houston's drive for the playoffs and had settled in well with his teammates. He was also earning the respect of his peers.

Yao dunks after being fouled by Los Angeles Lakers' Mark Madsen.

"He's a whole lot better than I thought he was," said Detroit Pistons center Ben Wallace, himself an All-Star. "I was surprised by his awareness on the court. When he caught the ball deep in the paint, he didn't waste time. When he caught it outside, he turned and faced up and was able to find the open guy [for a pass]. That was impressive for a guy 7'5"."

As impressive as Yao was on the court, his impact outside of it was astounding. His simple, three-letter name was already well-known throughout sporting—and other—circles. In

"He's a whole lot better than I thought he was. I was surprised by his awareness on the court."
—Detroit Pistons center Ben Wallace

Houston, he had made a dramatic impact. Rockets attendance was up 17 percent for the 2002–2003 season. In 2001–2002, a mere 0.5 percent of Houston's group ticket sales were to members of the city's Asian community, according to the Rockets. During Yao's rookie campaign, they rose to nearly 12 percent.

Fans at the Compaq Center could munch on egg rolls while sipping a Chinese beer. And many public-address announcements were made in both English and Mandarin.

The rest of the NBA was affected, too. More than 40 percent of the traffic on the NBA's Web site was from countries other than the United States. Worldwide NBA merchandise sales were up 35 percent, to a staggering $1.8 billion. In the global village that the NBA had become, thanks to the recent influx of international players, the growth couldn't all be attributed to Yao. But he was making a difference. When the Chinese Web site, Sohu.com, held an online chat with Yao, nine million people logged on. The league had fourteen different television deals in China, an increase of nine from the previous season.

Houston Rocket's Cuttino Mobley jumps on Yao Ming's back in celebration after the team defeated the Boston Celtics in overtime, 101-95, February 24, 2003.

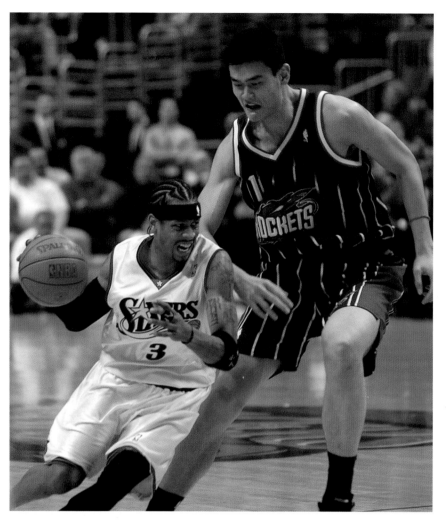

Philadelphia 76ers' Allen Iverson is dwarfed as he drives on Yao Ming.

"Yao is emerging as a cultural icon for a number of reasons," said NBA senior international vice president Andrew Messick. "The fact that he is from China and is very skillful and has a great personality [have] all contributed to his popularity."

The NBA wasn't the only source to benefit from Yao's growing reputation. The man himself had realized quite a windfall, although he wasn't necessarily impressed by it. "I think it's all pretty boring," he said. "I'd much rather be playing basketball." By the end of January, commercials had aired starring Yao selling Apple Computers and Visa. In February, he made a television spot for the sports drink Gatorade, which would debut in the summer of 2003. Yao had negotiated a pair of endorsement deals in China, one for a company that develops video games for mobile phones—a perfect fit for his own love of gaming—and the other for a wireless service provider. The group of financial advisers he had assembled, known as "Team Yao," had been extremely effective in *marketing* the rookie—and adding to his bank account. Yao had signed a four-year, $17.8 million contract with the Rockets. He was expected to make $4 million more in endorsements during the 2002–2003 season. Some in the advertising community thought the number could swell to $10 million in 2003–2004.

But the real story for Yao was on the court. He finished the 2002–2003 season averaging 13.5 points, 8.2 rebounds, and 1.8 *blocks* per game, and finished in the top 20 in eleven different statistical categories. The Rockets made a strong drive for the playoffs but ultimately missed out on the post-season. Yao finished second—to Phoenix forward Amare Stoudamire— in the Rookie of the Year voting. It was a tremendous season, one that featured an enormous amount of attention. In the end, though, Yao stood tall. He showed he could play ball and represent China in the NBA. It may have taken a while for it to happen, but Yao had succeeded.

A fan proclaims "The New Ming Dynasty"!

"The Chinese have never had [a professional] athlete succeed on the world stage," said Eric Zhang, Yao's closest advisor. "They've been waiting for someone like Yao. Now is his time."

And it had just begun.

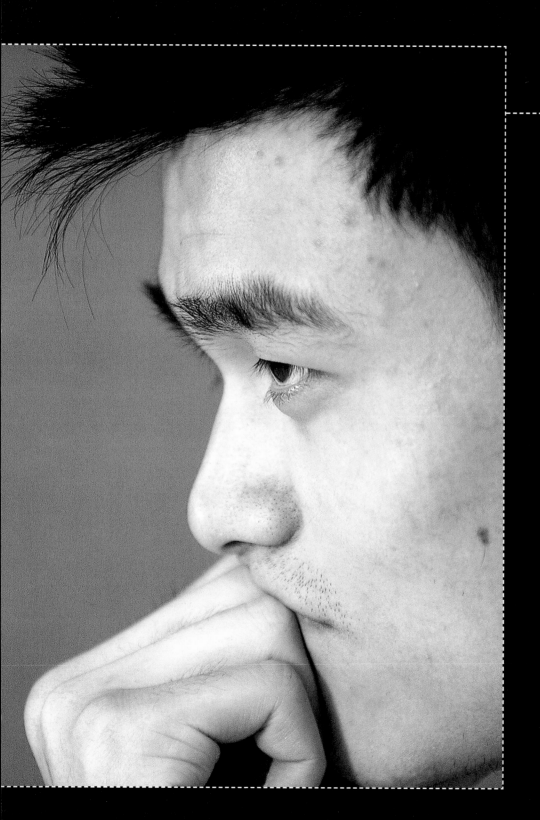

stats

Stats

Born: September 12, 1980
Birthplace: Shanghai, China
Height: 7'5" (228 cm)
Weight: 310 pounds (140.6 kg)
Team: Houston Rockets
Position: Center

Career Highlights

Year	Games	Games Started	Minutes per Game	Field Goal %
2002–2003	82	72	29.0	.498
2003–2004	17	17	34.9	.486

3-point %	Free Throw %	Rebounds Per Game (RPG)	Offense (RPG)	Defense (RPG)
.500	.811	8.20	2.40	5.80
.000	.769	9.60	2.90	6.70

Assists Per Game	Blocks Per Game	Points Per Game
1.7	1.79	13.5
1.9	2.06	17.2

Source: NBA.com (http://www.nba.com/playerfile/yao_ming/index.html?nav=page)
[2003–2004 stats as of 12/4/03]

GLOSSARY

avalanche—Anything that comes upon a person quickly and in large quantities.

block—The act of knocking an opponent's shot away from the basket. Players must block a shot on its way up toward the basket. If a player touches the ball as it heads down toward the hoop, the shooter is awarded two points, even if the ball wasn't likely to go in.

clearance—Official permission to do something.

crossover move—A maneuver made by a player who is dribbling the ball and attempts to pass a defender by shifting the ball from one hand to the other quickly, in the hopes of catching the opponent leaning too far in one direction and unable to react to the switch.

crucial—Extremely important.

cultural—Having to do with the ideas, customs, arts, and habits of a specific country or people.

execute—To carry out an assignment in a way that has been requested or demanded.

finger roll—A delicate shot at the basket, usually from inside five feet, in which the player tries to roll the ball off his fingertips and into the basket.

foul—Any error committed by a player in which he makes illegal contact with a member of another team.

franchise—A business in one area that is part of a larger company. In the NBA, there are thirty franchises throughout the country.

frontcourt—The name given to the two forwards and center on each team. They play closest to the basket and so are considered in the frontcourt. The two guards comprise the backcourt.

low post—The area close to the basket where taller players try to establish position, in the hope of getting an easy shot.

mandates—Direct orders given to individuals by those who are in charge.

marketing—The act of promoting a person, place, or thing by bringing the general public's attention to it.

perennial—Something that occurs every year. A team that makes the playoffs each year is known as a "perennial post-season club."

rebound—A missed shot at the basket that is grabbed, usually from the air, by a player from either team.

shot clock—A part of the scoreboard that lets players know how much time they have to shoot the ball each time they have it. In the NBA, teams must attempt a shot, which either goes in the basket or hits the rim, within twenty-four seconds. Failure to do that results in losing the ball.

tentative—Not confident of one's ability to do something. This also means plans that are made but could be changed later on.

three-pointer—A shot attempted from behind the arc that is painted on the court approximately twenty-three feet from the basket. A successful shot is worth three points for the team whose player sinks it. This is also called a "trey," a "trifecta," a "triple," or a "three ball."

turnover—The loss of possession of the ball to the other team, either by having it stolen or by dribbling or passing the ball out of bounds.

U.S. Dream Team—The nickname given to the players chosen to represent the United States in the Summer Olympics, beginning in 1992. Since the members of the team were among the best in the NBA, it was considered a squad so good one could only dream about actually putting it on the court.

FIND OUT MORE

Books

Choi, Douglas. *"Moving Great Wall" Yao Ming*. Seattle, WA: Almond Tree Books, LLC, 2003.

Hareas, John. *Yao Ming*. New York: Scholastic Paperbacks, 2003.

Pyle, Linda. *Yao Ming* (Awesome Athletes). Edina, MN: Abdo Publishing Co., 2003.

Web Sites

CBS Sportsline
http://www.cbs.sportsline.com/nba/players/playerpage/307933

ESPN
http://www.sports.espn.go.com/nba/players/profile?statsld=3599

National Basketball Association
http://www.nba.com/playerfile/yao_ming

INDEX

Page numbers in **boldface** are illustrations.